DID HE CHOOSE YOU

THE GUIDE TO IDENTIFYING THYSELF

AUTHOR

TAMARA CRAWFORD

CREATE YOUR DESTINY PUBLISHING LLC
244 Madison Ave Suite 1250
New York, NY 10016

USA

ISBN-13: 978-0-578-88165-2

Book Design by Tamara Crawford

Table of Content

Prelude

This book answers questions regarding who a woman loves and why she loves him. Are you with a man you love, but you wish he would make a few changes? Are you dating without a title? Does your man play games with you? Are you confused about your position in his life? This book focuses on why you choose the men you choose. You will learn all about your man, and hopefully, a little about yourself. I am not a licensed therapist. My infatuation with studying relationship patterns stems from my educational background. My bachelors and masters' degrees are both in psychology. The study of behavior has always intrigued me. The nature of human behavior is often repetitive and our need for love often incites a continuous pattern in relationships.

My interest in identifying patterns in women's behavior will provide insight on the men you consistently choose throughout your lifetime. Marriage is not at the top of the priority list for all women as it once was. Marriage is sometimes portrayed as more of a responsibility than an aspiration. More women are deciding to delay marriage and children, until their careers flourish. Relationships have evolved from the nineteenth century. Women are more independent now than ever before.

Multiple partner relationships are at an all-time high. The traditions and perception of relationships have drastically changed over the last decade. Love is inevitable, but is companionship and/or marriage to the right person? There is always a point in a woman's life when she falls in love. Sometimes, a woman will only fall in love once in her lifetime. Some women may fall in love multiple times, and others, never at all. The hope with dating is to meet someone that you can share your life with.

When a woman meets a man that has the potential to be her significant other, she has found a great thing, regardless of her perception of marriage. Every woman may differ in what it takes to allow a man in her heart, but there is always a way in. Single men are always a commodity to women because most women want marriage. Marriage is often not a priority for men. Some men want marriage eventually, and others may not want it at all. Many men want the benefits of a relationship without the restrictions.

When a woman meets a man, she is often unaware of his intentions. Her physical appearance is often what has piqued his interest. For men, physical attraction is the key to the beginning, and for women, it is often an emotional chemistry that connects them. What a woman wants from a man will determine what she is willing to do to get him.

What a man wants from a woman will determine what her purpose will be in his life. Pay attention to his purpose for you. You determine if his purpose matches yours. A relationship grows as you become more comfortable with your partner. Different individuals have different opinions on how a relationship should evolve. Although the whole dynamic of relationships has changed, women still want love. Non-exclusivity in relationships has become a social norm in society today.

The new age coined term for this is a *situationship*. A situationship is dating without a title. Situationships are never an issue, until they are. Women must be confident in their choices and decisions. Perception often justifies actions for most. Freedom in a relationship is necessary, but freedom to cheat is optional. Welcome to the journey of finding yourself, through the men you choose.

MESSAGE FROM YOUR AUTHOR

As women, we want perfection, when in actuality, no one is perfect, not even us. For a relationship to withstand the test of time, one must dedicate their time to the relationship for it to prosper. Throughout this book, you will learn, grow and hopefully, empower those around you. My knowledge is acquired through research in graduate school, personal experiences, wonderful associates, and from observations. This book is to be used as a reference to any of your relatable experiences. My aspiration in life is to help those around me, and knowledge is the best gift one could give. Enjoy!

HIM

Men are classified into nine categories in this book. There is *the Single man, the Prowler, the Playa, Mr. Trapped, the Married Man, the Sugar Daddy, the Ex, Mr. Co-dependent* and *your Dream guy.* You may be reading this book in a relationship or single. For either situation, you should know why you chose your man. You may be reading this book because you want to know who you are with. You may be reading this book to determine where you are in your relationship. It is important to know who you are before you can understand who you are with. Men decide who they are interested in.

Men decide who they want to propose to. A woman's value to a man is based on the value she has for herself. When you meet a man interested in you, he will most likely pursue you. Women often complain about their man's deficiencies. Perfection in a relationship is the fairytale that most women dream of. The reality is there is no perfect individual in the universe. The man of your dreams will not be perfect, but he will be the right man for you. The key to choosing the right man to share your life with is to know thyself. Many women overlook key elements in achieving a successful relationship while dating and focus on superficial things like how nice his car is.

Material things rarely indicate that a man is marriage material. Some women fall in love with the dream of who their man could be, instead of who he already is. Men can develop and grow, but it must be at their pace. The man that you choose to be in a relationship, situationship or marriage with, speaks volumes about you. You reflect your man, so who you entertain reflects how you view yourself. Every woman wants to be with the man she adores. There is a lot of controversy on the topic of whether who you love is optional. Regardless of if you think it is optional to love someone, you want love to be reciprocated. In some relationships, love is not always reciprocated. One person can be in love, and the other is simply in lust or just likes the person. When things are not equal, someone often feels mistreated.

Do you feel that your love is being reciprocated? Do you believe you are reciprocating love the same way? Men are extremely guarded when it comes to their heart. Women are the total opposite. Women often love repeatedly, learning different lessons in each love story. Men are logical thinkers, so falling in love repeatedly is irrational and seems unnecessary for them. Love rarely happens for men as easily, or as frequently as it does for women. A man's actions will depict the future that he wants with you.

When you read this book, you will be able to decipher who you are with, why you are with the man you are with, and if he is the one for you. Love with the right man is blissful. Love with the wrong man could be disastrous. The various men in this book are the men that you date, have children with, and marry. Commitment is a choice, and you choose your man. We will take a journey through your past, to an epiphany, and/or a breakthrough.

ACKNOWLEGEMENT

 This book is my first project, and as a new author, it was a gut-wrenching process to release it. I wanted perfection but during this process, I realized the book would never be perfect enough for me. My first life lesson for anyone reading this is that there is no such thing as perfection. All you can do is your best. Your best is always good enough. My fears delayed my book release. Confidence is truly golden, and believing in yourself is the key to your success. Never delay anything that you aspire to do. The time is always now. My friends have been asking me when I was going to publish this book and I would always say *soon*. Well guys, here it is. I hope you enjoy.

First and Foremost, I want to thank God for allowing me the opportunity to be a vessel of wisdom to those around me. To my high school guidance counselor, thank you for telling me that I could never graduate on time. You never understand why people are positioned in your path because hindsight is 20/20. You gave me the motivation to not only graduate from high school on time, but to attain two college degrees and well, become an author. To my mother, thank you for teaching me that only the strong survive. To my father, thank you for being my voice of reason.

My knowledge and experience in relationships have truly allowed me the ability to be a vessel. Every life lesson that I learned was imperative for me to be where I am today. It is my aspiration to build unity within African American families, so who better to begin with than my women. To my children, you are the light of my life, and everything that I aspire to do is to motivate you and make you proud. I thank God for you daily. To the man that never loved me, I learned so much through you, thank you. To my family, those that are distant and close, I appreciate all the life lessons. To everyone that believed in me, without you, this could not be possible. This is just the beginning.

CHAPTER ONE

The Single Man

When a woman begins dating a man that she is compatible with, there are often hopes for a relationship to blossom. This chapter embarks on the journey of dating a single man. Most women fantasize about relationships with single men. The only way to truly get a husband is to date a single man. Single men always seem to be a great catch to women because they are available. Almost all women want marriage and family at some point in life. You ask where the problem lies ladies? Well, some men are single because they want to be single. Some men are afraid of commitment and losing their freedom. Some women may become insecure if their man is afraid to commit. Some women present their concerns to their partner.

He may or may not resolve his woman's concerns. It truly may not have anything to do with you. He may just not be ready for a relationship and may not be willing to disclose why. When you reach a crossroad in your situationship, you will have to decide what is best for you, especially in the event that his actions are not fulfilling your needs. Marriage and Family Therapy is not regularly sought out prior to the beginning of romances.

Many people seek guidance when the relationship is in danger of failing. Individuals rarely focus on compatibility at first glance. A woman learns about her man while she dates him. A woman will only know her lover's previous experiences if he feels comfortable enough to divulge them. His past is the key to your future with him. If you are dating a man that is afraid of commitment, determine if you are willing to be patient until he is ready. All single men are not as transparent as women want them to be. Single men are often self-sufficient and independent, but not all. Some single men are co-dependent. Most women can decipher if she is dating an independent or co-dependent man. Some single men are more co-dependent than others.

Co-dependent men can be clingy in relationships with independent women. It is not your responsibility to identify why a man is not ready to commit or to pressure your significant other into a relationship. However, it is your responsibility to ask for what you need. If you ask for what you need, you will be able to determine if you can acquire what you want. Many women prefer an independent single man over a co-dependent single man. You can determine if you are dating a man that is co-dependent by monitoring how much time he spends with you. A single independent man will want his freedom.

A single co-dependent man will consume a lot of your time. This is the most effective way to determine if he is co-dependent. A man that is co-dependent tends to isolate you from others. These men are often unstable, have difficulties with finances and often need support with daily decisions. We will discuss co-dependent men in more detail later in this book. Women want to feel like they are being chosen over any other woman. Whether a man is single and independent or co-dependent, he will show you what he wants from you. Most women marry for love, some marry for stability and others marry for companionship. Relationships and titles coincide with responsibilities. If you decide to enter a relationship, you now have a title and there are roles associated with your title. Some women want the title but would rather not have the responsibility.

When a woman is ready for commitment, she will become vocal about it. If her man is not ready to commit when she is ready, it could cause problems within the union. Women find independence illuminating, so when single men exuberate a detached aura, he become more attractive. Do you know what your single man wants? Does he want marriage? Does he want children? Does he want a friend? Do you genuinely want marriage?

Some single men are honest and will let you know what they want. Others are not so honest. Men show you what they want from you through their dedication and commitment. Some men show interest when they first meet you, and their interest will continue to grow if they want a future with you. Other men may show a lack of interest, or only show interest in intimacy. His behavior teaches you everything you need to know about him. His actions coincide with his wants not his words. If a man is not interested in commitment, you will know. Men and women relatively think differently when it comes to dating. If men are not in committed relationships, they often date more than one woman at a time. Women usually only date one man at a time. Women rarely date multiple men at once.

Most men believe that if a man has not discussed commitment, dating other women is optional. Some men date other women while in committed relationships. You know who your man is though. Expectations vary regarding relationships. Some women believe that men should be allowed to date other women if they are not in a committed relationship. Some women want the man to date just them. Some women may want a man to commit as soon as they become intimate.

Communication is imperative in a relationship. Intimacy is an uncomfortable topic. It is important to discuss intimacy before being intimate. It provides an open dialogue on an important topic. Men may be intimate with more than one woman at a time. Often, women are aware if their guy is intimate with more than one woman at a time. Some women initially indicate that it does not matter if her man is intimate with other women and later complain about his indiscretions. Some women may truly not be aware. You must be decisive in your standards. Men are often decisive with theirs. There are men with double standards, who expect women to only date them while they date multiple women. There are also men that will criticize women for exhibiting the same behavior that men engage in.

Some women will only date one man while he dates other women. Other women live by the same standard as their man. Marriage is not necessary for procreation but is pertinent for two-parent households. Many women want the finished product without the work. The lines of dating can get blurred if you are not honest about your intentions. A relationship is not a chess games. It is not about strategy and moves.

If you are not honest with your intentions, he will not be honest with his. Even if he is dishonest about his intentions, you should still be honest about yours. Lead by the example that you want to set in your relationship. This does not mean that you condone dishonesty, only that you expect integrity. One only has power over themselves. If you want a relationship and your beau is not ready to commit, what are your options? Well, there are quite a few options. You can wait until he is ready. You can sever ties. You could also monitor the progression of your relationship. Here is an example: If you have been dating a man for six months, and he is secretive and you have not met his family, you may want to ask him where the relationship is going? He could be playing games with you. You will learn about the game in a later chapter.

Men that are not ready to commit often make excuses about commitment. His excuses do not mean that he is not interested in you. He just may not be ready for all the responsibility that comes with a relationship. He must be ready for a relationship before he commits. If he is not ready and is pressured into commitment, the relationship could end poorly. How you get him is how you may lose him, so be mindful of your actions.

Holidays are also a key to identify where your relationship is going. If he is inviting you to Christmas dinner with his family, he may be ready to commit. Although some single men may not be searching for exclusivity, many men are. Some women go through extreme measures to get the man she wants. Since many men are afraid of commitment, women must practice patience if she genuinely wants him. Patience will allow you the time you need to determine if the man you are with is the man that you want to share a lifetime with. The ability to ascertain what you want and expect from a man should align with his wants and needs. Women, when you meet a man, you should treat him as if he will be your husband. If you treat him as you want to be treated, things will flow naturally.

Circumstances sometimes interfere with a man's ability to be what a woman needs. Trust can sometimes interfere when it comes to commitment. Women sometimes notice what their friends are experiencing in relationships, and it could influence their decisions within their own relationships. It is never your fault if a man is unable to commit to you, unless you are playing the game. For him to make you his wife, honesty and loyalty are often required to go to the next level.

If you play 'the game' when you begin dating him, he may be reluctant to take things to the next level because he may not trust you. You may think you want a relationship but may later realize that you just wanted a companion. Never allow anyone to rush you into anything that you are not ready for. You will know if it is the right time with the right person if you are taking your time to assess if your man meets your criteria. Some women believe in fate and kismet, while others believe in strategy and logic. A relationship and a family are wonderful, but make sure that you are read and that it is with the right person. Men are often not as communicative as women. Men have difficulties being vulnerable. Some men may feel that being single is safer than being in a relationship. If you are in a situationship, you must decide how long is too long to wait for a commitment.

If you are dating and you have been with him for more than a year, it could be time to move on. Women are mainly monogamous by nature, so dating more than one man at a time is uncommon. Women are not usually intimate with more than one man at a time while some men utilize intimacy as a ploy to get what they want. Women have different expectations than men. Intimacy typically solidifies the relationship for women. Men are a bit different.

Intimacy does not solidify the deal for men. Women are emotional creatures and intimacy creates a bond that may cloud their judgment. Men look beyond the emotional connection and into the future with the individual. If a man is unable to see growth with a woman; they typically continue to search for what they want. Many women want their man to be transparent with his intentions. Some men will engage in relationships that are leading nowhere fast. Misleading people is wrong. Being forthright and honest is imperative. Some women hurt themselves trying to make a man love them. Love must come naturally to survive the test of time. If you are dating a single man and you are questioning your place or value, you may want to re-evaluate your needs.

If you try to force a relationship, you may most likely hurt yourself in the process. The importance of a mutual understanding is imperative to happiness. Many women that have pursued men rarely brag about their accolades. There is nothing wrong with allowing a man to know that you are interested in him. It is something else to try to force commitment on him. It almost always leads to resentments. The guy that you are dating may be the one for you. You must understand that you will have what is for you.

You do not have to chase a relationship, manipulate it, argue about it or apply any pressure to obtain it. A relationship must be something he wants. If you are unhappy waiting for someone to commit to you, learn what will make you happy. Your well-being and happiness should always be the most important thing to you. Lesson 1: Love yourself enough to set standards. If a man wants you, he will comply.

It is easier to blame someone else for your mistakes than to blame yourself. People need freedom, regardless of if they want a relationship or not. If a man is not willing to commit due to trust issues while playing the game, you may have to press the reset button. If he is the one for you, you will have him.

Some women require a timeframe for a man to commit. Others refuse to wait on a man to decide to commit. Regardless of which woman you are, you have choices. The most important lesson to learn about relationships is that they are continuous work, and the effort is endless. What you put in is what you will receive. If you allow him time to commit, and he commits to you, you will be happy you were patient. If he never commits to you, you will feel as though you have wasted your time. If you choose to leave, you will have to start over.

Most women hate starting over and will remain in meaningless relationships. Starting over is always scary but sometimes necessary. In business, without risk, you reduce the possibility of obtaining a reward. In relationships, if you are not willing to take the risk, you risk losing it all anyway. You must decide what you want, and what is worth fighting for. You must decide if you are wasting your time of he is worth being patient for. His actions will reflect his intentions. Key 1: Some men are charming, which women may confuse for intentional action. If his words are empty, you can confirm that through his actions. You just need to pay attention. Example: If your beau ignores your calls or is unwilling to commit; he may not be the guy for you. Time is precious, and you must treat yours a such.

Self -worth is important even in dating. Some women complain that they lose themselves in their relationships. Two years of dating without commitment will rarely result in commitment. A title is mainly for validation purposes, but your wants should be granted after being with someone for two years. If your beau wants you, he knows how to find you. Many women waste their time with the wrong guy. When you give a man space, he should realize what you mean to him. Absence is supposed to make your man fantasize about you.

If he is out with someone else instead, he is probably not the man for you. You can never make a man happy if you are unhappy with yourself. Any man that wants you in his life will not allow you to walk away from him. You may kiss a few imposters before you meet your husband. Your husband will not have an issue with committing to you. If he is not committing to you, he does not see a future with you. It could also be that you are the woman that he wants to be with, but he is not yet ready to settle down. Some men associate commitment with confinement. If your man feels like this, you may need to evaluate your insecurities. You will lose him if you smother him too much. Women are often ready for commitment before a man is.

Commitment should happen organically. Things happen when they are supposed to happen, not when you want them to. Timing is everything in a relationship. Your happiness should be the most important thing to you. If you are not happy in the space you are in, you must re-evaluate that space. You are beautiful, and you are kind. You deserve the world. If the man that you are with does not provide that, he is not the man for you. When you transition from dating to being single, there are some things you should take with you. You should always remember to take your self-worth. You should always remember to take your dignity.

If a man does not realize your worth, then it is his loss. Many women date one man at a time instead of multiple men. There is a negative stigma associated with women dating multiple men at a time. Therefore, many women fall for the first man they begin dating after a break-up. This is often called the rebound guy. Every woman has dated a man after a breakup from a long-term relationship. Oftentimes, when you focus on yourself, you end up realizing your mistakes. You know if a guy is what you are looking for when you meet him. All women have criteria. Your selection is your selection. You must learn why you continue to encounter similar situations when it comes to dating. When you meet a new guy, be honest with him.

Honesty will build a solid foundation and gain respect from him. Tell your new beau everything you are looking for in a man and refuse to settle for anything less. You do not have to discuss your previous relationships. They are not important. You never want your new man to think about your ex. Whenever you start over, never look at it as a bad thing. Typically, when things end with a guy, it is for good reason. You time is precious, and so are your experiences. Dating a single man can go countless ways. The fun part about life is that we are unable to determine the future. If you are dating, and you are single, enjoy yourself.

You can only be a victim if you want to be a victim. Loving someone else is always about loving you first. Do not offer something that is not being reciprocated. Loving yourself first will allow you to receive the best love possible. If you are receiving this love from your single man, then your relationship will progress and flourish into something beautiful. Trust the process.

CHAPTER TWO

The Prowler

Who is a prowler? The prowler is an attractive guy that preys on women. When a woman meets a prowler, she rarely is aware that he is a prowler. Most often, prowlers are men that are unstable. The instability could be due to indecisiveness and/or lack of confidence. Prowlers may also not be single. Some of these men are in healthy relationships. Prowlers are portrayed as men that take advantage of women. These men ask women for their assistance with improving their lives. Prowlers often prey on women with self-esteem issues. All women have bouts with self-esteem. Women can struggle with bouts of self-esteem from hair textures to weight issues, intellect or/etc. Women may feel insecure as a result of previous partners, parents or their environment which is nothing to be ashamed of.

If you are reading this, and realize that you are dating a prowler, you are in a better position than before. Being aware is always better than being unaware. Prowlers prey on weaknesses, so if you are divulging your deepest darkest secrets, then there is a possibility that he may use the knowledge against you and to his advantage.

Prowlers tell women what they want to hear. If a woman needs a man to show her attention or tell her that she is beautiful, he will fulfill those fantasies. If a woman needs a man in the home as a father figure, most prowlers will leap at the opportunity. You can identify a prowler by what he is doing. Is he rushing to move in, get married or have a family when you guys have just gotten together? You may want to consider where his exes are? Where are you financially? Are you in a position to elevate him? Why are his exes no longer interested in him? Why is he so into you? Most women love a good catch, but you need to determine if your catch should be thrown back in the pond. Does he contribute to your life or he is always in need? Ladies, you can tell if you are dating a prowler by what he asks you. If he is asking more than he is offering, you have a problem. Lesson 2: A man should come to the table with something for the table.

Some men may have setbacks in life due to circumstances. This does not mean that you should not support your man. It is important to pay attention and to not be manipulated into helping a man that uses women to their advantage. Relationships are about teamwork. Relationships are not just about one individual being committed. If this is your relationship, you may want to re-evaluate what you are gaining from it.

Prowlers have multiple women catering to the same needs. These men may live with one woman and have another woman managing his bills, another caring for his daily needs, etc. These men can also be portrayed as womanizers. These guys are typically emotionally detached and have a fear of true intimacy. Some prowlers will never fully commit, while others may get tired of the game. Karma is charismatic at first glance, but later implodes the lesson necessary for growth through mistakes. The key to learning is to recognize why you are dating who you are dating, and how it relates to where you are in your life.

A man can have every woman believe that she is the only woman.

Key 2: If you do not pay attention to the signs that a man shows you, your heartache is a choice you made. His vibe will tell you everything you need to know. You must pay attention. Some women get upset with the world when a man hurts them. If you do this, you are not learning or growing, and this will only hinder you. Growth is necessary in the process of love. Women often blame men for their actions when women must take some accountability. What role did you play? Did you set your standards, or did he set the standard? These are things that women typically ask themselves when the relationship is over. Ladies, it is important to ask these questions while in the relationship.

When you are getting to know a man, it is important to leave your past in the past. You need to get to know a guy before you start letting him in on every detail of your life. A man's interest is not as important as your standards are. Allow a man to learn your likes and dislikes. Learn to be more elusive. Men like to chase women. Men are rarely interested in the women chasing them. When women date prowlers, they are often doing most of the chasing. If you chase a man, he will most likely lose interest. A man that is interested in you will invest his time and energy in you. You will not have to beg, borrow or steal for it. It is easy to be deceived by a prowler if you are not paying attention to his actions. I will continuously repeat this throughout the book.

His actions will show you everything you need to know about him. Prowlers will be geared more towards selfish innuendos. The prowler is not seen as the worst man in the world to date. He is an opportunist. If the next best thing appears, he may be moving on without you. A person can only do what you allow, so only allow what you want. If you are in a relationship with a prowler, you may want to ask yourself, why you are there. If this man does not put the same effort into the relationship as you do, he may not be the one for you. A man that loves you will try his best to make you happy.

He will not take your kindness for weakness, nor will he try to take advantage of you. You matter. If you are dating a prowler, and he is unwilling to obtain synergy, trust the process. Being alone is always better than being used or feeling miserable. If you are in love with a prowler and you feel like you are being taken advantage of, stop letting him take advantage of you. It is just that simple. Set some boundaries in your relationship if you want to stay. If you stop catering to him, he will move on.

Prowlers are often in the relationship for the perks, so if there are none, then there is no need to remain in the relationship. A higher power does things that one is unable to do for themselves. Only you can determine if your prowler makes you happy. Everyone around you is affected by your relationship. Your happiness is often displayed, so if you are unhappy, others will notice. You must decide what is best for you. Being unhappy is an option that you do not have to choose. A man is supposed to make you happy not sad. He should fulfill your dreams and fantasies while you fulfill his. If a relationship is one-sided, then you are in it alone. You teach someone how to love you. The way you love yourself is the key to a long-lasting relationship with someone else. A man that loves you will show you.

He will show you through his discernment, his loyalty, his dedication, admiration, commitment and faithfulness. A prowler will not be able to provide you with all the above. He will repeatedly fall short. He will be selfish, dishonest, and often condescending. If you are dating a prowler, determine why? If you are unable to identify why, then you are wasting time. Life is too short to be unhappy. A woman that is confident in her relationship should be able to easily determine her man's actions and whether she is happy. If you are confused about his actions, then you are confused about your relationship. Some women fall for a prowler, because they appear to be the ideal man, but looks can be deceiving. For you to receive love, you must be open, and ready for it. Many gestures appear to be love, but are they genuinely love? Remember that a man is going to invest in a woman that he loves. A woman should never fall in love with monetary gestures.

She should fall in love with his consideration, compassion and his commitment. What a man does for you is important. Men that are willing to stop everything for you if they are committed to you. Men only want to make women that they want to be with happy. If a man is not doing everything he can, he is not the man for you. There are many unhappy women playing the role of a man's mother instead of his potential wife.

Being a wife is a big responsibility, and one should want the title, not acquire it. Make sure that you are making choices for your life and not your prowler. If you want more from your partner, you can have it. You must ask him for it. He has the option to provide you what you require. Women spend a lot of time in the wrong relationship because of the fear of starting anew. Your happiness matters. Who else's happiness is more important than yours? You must stand for something or will likely fall victim to almost . Loving yourself is the key to your happiness. If you are secure within yourself, it will be difficult for a prowler to manipulate you. You will expect too much from him and it will deter him from pursing you. Prowlers rarely want to work hard for a woman, so you can spot them a mile away. They tend to look for the women to do all the work in the relationship, which can leave you drained.

Ladies, if you must do all the work in your relationship, you are not in the right relationship. A woman should never have to put in all the effort, and her man should never want her to. If your prowler has not changed by the time you figure out, he is a prowler, and it may be best to let him go. Being used is optional and being loved is intentional. If you are dating a prowler and decide to stay, set boundaries to protect yourself. Decide if you want a man that watches your efforts but is unwilling to put forth any effort. The effort that you provide should be the effort that you receive. A prowler can become your husband. He will decide if he wants you as a wife, but you will be aware of his choice. The prowler that decides to become a husband is the man that realizes he has found his prize. You are worth his effort, and he will understand that he could lose you without it. Have him show you that he is worthy of your time. You have a lot to offer. You must believe it. A man will choose how he treats you, based on how you treat yourself. If you are good to yourself, he will always be good to you. Keep that in mind and set your standards high.

CHAPTER THREE

The Playa

The playa is different from the men in the other categories. The playa will most often captivate you. The playa usually steals his woman's heart. When you meet a playa, he will almost always tell you that he is not interested in a relationship. Most women will not even care. The playa is often a single guy and marriage is rarely on his radar. If you are involved with a playa, be ready to deal with an abundance of drama. These men are most often eligible bachelors. Why, you ask? They are independent, usually established, and most often, emotionally detached. The emotional detachment is what attracts women to these men. Their aloofness is also appealing to women.

There are three types of playas. You have the established playa, the preyer playa and the user playa. The established playa is the man that every woman wants. He has it all. He is smart, educated, family oriented and driven. Often, established playas come into the situation with an agenda. These men want something superficial. They may be too consumed with their own lives or work to focus on a relationship. Your man may have been hurt in the past and is afraid of the constraints of a relationship.

These men rarely give compliments so you will always strive to impress him. This could leave a woman feeling unworthy, which may affect her self-esteem. In a relationship, a man should make you feel valued, appreciated and adored. If you are with an established playa, you feel underappreciated or mistreated. These men often make excuses when it comes to spending time with you. They keep their distance to wedge a distance between you. The second type of playa is the preyer playa. The preyer playa is a man that preys on vulnerable women. Preyer playas like women that are fresh out of a relationship or with some clear dependencies. They will boost a woman's ego like prowlers. These men know how to make a woman feel good, needed and wanted, but will require a lot of support. Identify who you are with.

All women want the happily ever after fairy tale. Sometimes, women have a difficult time deciphering what they are truly yearning for. A relationship should only take place with someone that complements you. A complement is a term of endearment. A man that complements you will bring out the best in you. He will make you feel empowered, supported and enlightened. It is important to spend some time by yourself before entering a new relationship. If not, you may become susceptible to falling for the wrong guy.

If you just met a guy, and he is ready to elope and move in together, you may want to ask yourself why. Some preyer playas implement marriage and family in their scheme. The user playa is like the preyer playa. The only difference is the user playa will use you until you have nothing left to offer. Ladies, men are logical thinkers and are often more carefree than women. Your feelings are not on his priority list. User playas monitor women's behavior to determine their actions. They rarely want a woman that cannot take them to the next level. User playas are illuminatingly dangerous. A man trying to achieve greatness is a blessing. If he attempts to manipulate you to achieve greatness, determine if he is merely using you for his advantage.

A connection is just that, a connection. A playa's plan to achieve greatness may come with or without you. He may only want to use you to reach a certain milestone in his life. He may be with you forever. You and your playa may connect, but on what level? Is your playa willing to stop playing and settle down with you, or is he always seeking the next best opportunity? Playas are often desirable, yet often truly unattainable. Playas are typically not concerned about their partners. Playas are typically too consumed with themselves to focus on a relationship. These men tend to be selfish. His decision to commit is solely up to him.

If a playa is ready for commitment, he will consider you. If a playa considers you, he will include your finances, your family and your livelihood. A playa rarely asks you to spend your money. The playa will invest his life and future with you if he wants to take the relationship to the next level. If he does not invest in you, then he is not invested in you long term. Take some time to identify his actions. Women like to blame men for everything and rarely accept responsibility for any contribution to the problem. A man can lie to you but if you have evidence of deceit, what do you do with it? Do you suppress it or ignore it? If you learn your man is a playa, and you decide to make it work, you must accept knowledge of his behavior.

Many women fall in love with a playa. There is no need to be ashamed if you are in love with a playa. Most playas are extremely manipulative. All women fall victim to some sort of manipulation in life. The rules of the game are to play or be played. All women will endure some heartache in their lifetime. The heartache will not last a lifetime. You will learn and grow through your heartache. By the end of the relationship, you will understand the game and have a respect for it. If you perceive yourself as a victim, you will always be a victim.

If you understand that you were merely a student in the lesson of love, you can evolve from your heartache. Some women become playas after experiencing heartache in their lifetime. Is this you? Are you playing the game to protect yourself from pain? If so, decide how long you are willing to play this game. Also, think about the karma associated with the games that you are playing. Some men cannot live with a bruised ego. It is better to be honest rather than play games, unless you are ready for the games that you may have to endure. You should never have to wait on a man to treat you the way you deserve to be treated. Your expectations are your standards, and you have the right not to settle for less. Here are a few ways to identify that you are dating a playa.

He will often keep his phone on vibrate. His phone tends to ring uncontrollably. He tends to ignore calls when you are around. He guards his phone with his life and is often illusive. Many playas make excuses on why they are unable to commit. The playa may indicate that your insecurities prevent him from entering a relationship with you. These are often excuses to buy time. Be wary of a man exhibiting these signs to you.

If your playa has a child and reminisces over his relationship with the mother of this child, he may not be fully over her. If he is not over someone else, how can he commit to you? If he tells you that you can see other people, he is not searching for exclusivity. A man that is fully ready to commit will not make excuses, he will commit. Some women will enter a relationship with a man that dates multiple women and get upset if he does not commit when she is ready.

If he is not ready to commit, you must allow him the time he needs to find what he is searching for. It is not for you to decide what is right for him. If you are not his first choice, any commitment acquired often ends the way it begun. He could absolutely love someone else and marry you. Sometimes in life, people settle for those that love them instead of being with the individual they love. Why is this, you ask? Well, not everyone seizes the opportunity when in it, and once it fades, trust and pride tend to surface and love loses. If you are with a man that loves someone else, you must decide if it is at the cost of your happiness. If you love someone else, you should allow your man the freedom to move on. You should only accept what you offer. In life, many people settle for a man to attain a title.

Why marry if you are not truly in love? Some women/men marry for stability. My first marriage was loveless. When you marry for the wrong reasons, you divorce for the right ones. It is important to be intentional with your actions. Never allow anyone to persuade you into something that you are not ready for, and vice versa. Some women marry for the perception of happiness and companionship. Sometimes, the marriage survives, and other times, the marriage fails. If your needs are not met, you will not be happy. For your needs to be met, you must communicate what you need. Women that fail to communicate their needs will never obtain what they need.

Women often fall in love hard and fast. Women often react on emotions, unlike men that utilize insight. If the only thing that he is providing you is intimacy, your relationship may be surrounded by lust. Lust is the physical chemistry between two individuals. Lust often evolves, but in some instances, it does not. You must be able to identify what kind of situation you are in. A man will always want to reap your benefits, even when he is not ready to stop playing.

Some men are selfish. Let us not crucify him for wanting to acquire his wants. Allow us to identify the position that you play in his repetitive behavior. Standards are your expectations. Is he treating you according to your standards? He should prioritize your wants and needs. If your playa is unable to provide you with what you need, then you may require some space. Your playa may need time to decide if you are the woman that he wants in his life.

Why be unhappy because someone else is unable to fulfill something you need? You must be able to fulfill your own wants, while he attempts to find what he needs. Your life is precious. You could spend more time focusing on exceling in your life. You must determine what your purpose is. If a man is ever confused about what he wants with you, make things simpler for him. Some people struggle in relationships, but for what?

You only suffer if you want to suffer. You determine what you want in your life. Even if you feel that there is no way out, there is always a way out. Lesson 3: You want to be his first choice, not his last option. You will be able to determine if you are an option by the way he treats you. Playas are often excited by the yearning need that his women have for him. This is often why he makes himself so unavailable for women. His unavailability increases the interest in the women that are pursuing him.

Watch his actions. He will show the most interest in the woman that is not pursuing him at all. Men love a challenge. Men may differ but monitor his behavior. You will notice that when the playa settles down, it will be with the woman that refused to settle. Many men rarely like titles because it limits them to what kind of behavior is acceptable. If you are in a committed relationship, it is not acceptable to post other women on your social media. If you are single, you are free to do as you like, but there may be backlash if you are dating. Some men parade other women to make their women insecure. Some playas are more discreet with their actions.

Social media has changed the way people interact. It has become easier to identify if your man is dating other women. If your man has an active social media account, you can locate all the women interested in your beau. Social media can create insecurity and chaos in a relationship. Many women develop resentment if she is providing her playa, with benefits of a relationship without the title. If you are in this situation, what are you gaining? He is not to be blamed for what he is offering. If you are just realizing that you are dating a playa, confront him about his indiscretions. Identify if therapy is an option to assist with his commitment issues. If not, identify what you want.

A man does not realize that he must change unless he feels the need to change. A man that does not want to lose his woman will make the necessary changes to keep her. If the playa has a nonchalant attitude, his actions will speak volumes. Your playa will show you what he wants. Life is full of various roads to travel. The path you chose will determine if your road is bumpy or smooth. You chose your route and where it leads. You can be on the road to paradise or hanging off the edge of a cliff. You can choose the path but are unable to determine the outcome of your choice. If you are in a relationship with a playa and want him to stop playing, do not play with him.

If you are in a relationship with a playa and you are unhappy, it is probably best to identify what will make you happy. There is no need to be in a relationship where you are being deprived of happiness. The depiction of love is learned in childhood. Your playa's childhood experiences may influence his capacity to reciprocate love as an adult. Therapy will provide a safe space to present issues that may interfere with your growth. Some men were taught to cheat. Therefore, you should never seek happiness from a man. It is not your responsibility to re-\program a man with poor behavior.

If you are unhappy, then what are you doing? Make sure that you are with someone that makes you happy. If you are arguing more than laughing, you may need to re-evaluate your relationship. A playa will always be a playa. It is not your responsibility to get him to stop playing. He must be ready to stop. If you attempt to be anything other than his companion, you will be providing him more than what is being requested. You are only in your situation for a companion. If titles have not been incorporated, you must respect your union. If you decide you want something more, you must express that. Do not allow the playa to play you. You decide what you want in your life. You only accept what you want.

Your mind, body and time are not at his discretion. Set boundaries and standards. There are keys to attaining a prosperous relationship, and respect is at the top of the list. You must respect each other. Your man should make you feel like his queen, and there can only be one queen on the throne at a time. If he is unable to give you the love you deserve, he does not deserve you. If your playa has met his match in you, he will show it by his willingness to provide you with what you need.

CHAPTER FOUR

Mr. Trapped

Mr. Trapped is the guy to be afraid of. Mr. Trapped is rarely honest about his feelings and is often looking to trap you. Mr. Trapped is usually emotionally unavailable, but extremely emotional and controlling. Mr. Trapped often has unresolved issues with love. You must be ready for love to get it. Mr. Trapped wants love, but has difficulties reciprocating it. How do you determine if you are dating Mr. Trapped? Ask Mr. Trapped where he sees himself in two years. Mr. Trapped will be unable to discuss the future because he lives in the past. Mr. Trapped appears to be emotionally available and single. He often has multiple women like the men in other categories.

A major difference between Mr. Trapped and the other categories is that Mr. Trapped sabotages his own relationships. He is often deflective and dismissive to those that try to understand him. Mr. Trapped initially appears to be a good catch to women. He is usually attractive, has decent employment and is often charismatic. He is often shallow and requires instant gratification.

Mr. Trapped often wants to be portrayed as the hero in the relationship but is vastly not present in it. Many women marry trapped men. Some trapped men are verbally and physically abusive. It is prevalent for control to be attained by this man. Mr. Trapped often views things from a traditional aspect and stresses gender roles in a relationship. He will point out your flaws and expect perfection from you. He will insist you follow his lead. Men are to lead the marriage, but not the woman. If you beau is attempting to control your every move and does not listen to understand you, he may be trapped. Mr. Trapped is often set in his ways and has difficulties with change. Now that you know who Mr. Trapped is, are you in a relationship with a man that is trapped? If so, are you happy in your relationship?

Do you see a future with this man? Are you growing together or growing apart? Mr. Trapped is often afraid for you to grow because he is afraid to grow. His need for dependency from women fulfills him. Some women are indecisive and need support with decisions. Some women are in a position of power at work and want their man in control at home. Mr. Trapped will be more compatible with a woman that needs his support rather than a woman that is self-sufficient. Some men need to feel needed, while others rarely require it.

You must know what you want from the man that you are with. If you have just realized that you are dating a man that is trapped, you must decide if he is right for you. Many women allow the man to choose them. You have every right to choose the man that you want in your life. If Mr. Trapped brings you joy, and is willing to commit, then you should commit. Remember that you must live with the decisions that you make. If Mr. Trapped is in anyway toxic, you must address the toxicity. If you are not able to address the issues one on one, you may need to seek answers through therapy. It is ultimately up to you. Your happiness is at stake. Life is meant to be lived happily. If your life is anything other than happy, you have some work to do. There is no longer a negative stigma related to therapy. Therapy often assists individuals with identifying barriers to growth within a relationship.

Many people consider therapy before marriage to ensure the union is ready for that step. If your man is unwilling to go to therapy, and the relationship is not progressing, what are your options? Well, you choose your own options. You must determine what you want in your life and what you expect from your partner. You ultimately decide what will be on your roadmap of life. Some women love trapped men because he provides a sense of security that other men are unable to.

The security provided by your man is centered on the co-dependency offered in this relationship. For some women, his security will ignite a feeling of togetherness that may be unattainable with others. Mr. Trapped is attentive to your needs. Some women may perceive Mr. Trapped as their soulmate. Your soul partner is your soul partner. Many often perceive a soul partner as an intertwined spirit that has been placed on this earth just for them. My thoughts are that everyone does indeed has a soul partner, and your soul partner will fulfill all your needs without mention. Everything you love, they will love. Everything you believe in, they will believe in. Everything that you dream about, they will want to attain for you, and vice versa. If you do not feel these with an individual, he is not your soul partner. The relationship with your soul partner will be different from any other relationship that you will ever have. This man will most likely portray everything you want in a man, until he does not.

Mr. Trapped most often portrays a persona that he is unable to maintain. His dependency will often consume some women and suffocate others. Many women that date trapped men prefer fantasy over reality. The perception of ignorance being bliss is intended to release women from the realities of their situation.

Are you with a trapped man and find yourself ignoring the late text to his phone or the late work hours? Are you happy? You must decide that. Are you fulfilled? If not, you have some decisions to make. If you are happy do what makes you happy. Some women understand that men may stray but tend to remain loyal. The theory that all men stray is a just a theory. Women know when their man is straying. The question that women find uncomfortable is, *does it matter?* Most women rarely condone cheating, but do they remain in their relationship? Relationships can be stringent based on the individuals in them.

A woman can only be expected to control herself in a relationship, but what your partner does matters. It is important to be proactive so that you do not have to be reactive. Speak about the uncomfortable conversations that will determine your future. Your roadmap is your destiny. Every decision that you make matters. Set standards and boundaries to ensure Mr. Trapped is unable to manipulate you into a trap.

Mr. Trapped is not the only man that has potential to stray. Mr. Trapped may be one of the only ones that will bring drama to your doorstep. His love for himself most times outweighs his love for others. Selfishness often concedes to arrogance. Monitor the signs that your man is displaying. This man will not be honest.

You may also find that he is not accountable in the relationship and blames his partner for everything. This relationship could be toxic if the two people in it are not tending to the other person's needs. Determine if you are just meeting his needs or if he is just meeting yours. Either way could be a disaster. Both parties must feel fulfilled. Many women rarely know exactly what they want in a man. Some women fall in love with the idea of what they want in a man. Many women argue with men to attempt to change things about them and vice versa. If you are arguing with a man to change his behavior, it only works if he wants to stop the behavior. His love for you must outweigh his need for adoration.

Your love for him will have to allow you to forgive his indiscretions. In life, people are not perfect. He just must be perfect enough for you. If Mr. Trapped is perfect for you, then Mr. Trapped is perfect for you. If Mr. Trapped is anything but perfect for you, is that good enough for you? Time is something precious and cannot be given back. Ultimately, your happiness should be the most important thing in your life. Marriage is only for individuals willing to withstand the test of time. Some people in marriage suffer when their marriage is not based on truth. Some can live with the ignorance and other are unable to. Everyone is different.

Our differences are what make us special and unique. Your uniqueness is what sets you apart from your partner but should also be what brings you together. Your differences should strengthen the relationship. Trust is the key to building a solid foundation. You will find yourself in a good place to make conscious decisions if you can trust your partner. If your relationship is built on anything other than trust, it may not survive.

You must trust the choices you make. If you trust every choice you make, how could you go wrong? Therefore, you must always set the tone. If you fail to set the tone, you have done yourself a disservice. If he can set the tone in your relationship, he will. It is his role to be clear with his intentions. He can only provide you what you allow. Envision the life you want for yourself. The life that you want for yourself is more important than the life that Mr. Trapped wants for you.

Be confident in what you want, so that you are not easily persuaded into what someone else wants for you. Remember that you decide your fate, not your loved one. Women get upset when they feel their time has been wasted, but you decide how your time is spent. If you are suffering in a relationship, emotionally or physically, then the relationship is not worth your time unless your partner changes from being selfish to self-less.

Women have suffered for decades, and many are still not as appreciated as they should be. Respect is not always given; it is often acquired. Will it cost your self-worth or your dignity? Women fought a long and hard battle to be treated equally, but in their homes, many are not treated as such. Men are not psychic and rarely understand what their women want. If you ask a man what his woman wants, he will tell you what he thinks she wants. Many men fail to identify what their women want. Usually, what you want, and need are two different things. For a man to understand what you need, his connection with you must be beyond words. A man will sell you a dream if you allow him to. If your man is truly unclear on what you need, then he clearly does not need you. Your needs and wants are important, and the man that you dedicate your time with should understand that.

He should dedicate his life to making you happy. If his goal is not to focus on your happiness, then you are not his choice. If making you happy does not make him happy, his intentions are not pure. If a man complains about doing things to make you happy, he is doing things for the recognition or reward. How often do men do something for nothing? How often do women? A man that genuinely wants you will not complain about doing things to make you happy.

He will love to do things to make you happy. This man will be attentive to your needs by listening to you. You must live with your partner, so ultimately, you must decide what is for you. People that look back on their lives regret the things that they never did. You must make the most appropriate choices in your life for yourself. Your example of how you love yourself will show him how you need to be loved, and if he loves you, he will be able to provide that love.

CHAPTER FIVE

The Married Guy

When we discuss the married guy in this book, we are not discussing men that have separated from their spouse. In this book, we will mainly discuss the dishonest married men. Many married men are honest, and others are not. My role is not to judge, but to explore them both. There are a few reasons that you may be dating a married man. He may have hidden the fact that he is married. He may be assisting you financially. He may have told you that things are complicated in his marriage. He may have indicated that he will be leaving his wife soon. Regardless of the reason, you must identify what you expect to gain from this relationship. If you are dating a married man that is still involved with his wife on some level, it will almost always be accompanied by some drama.

Let us classify married men into a few categories. There are married men that are not planning on leaving their wife. These men like to engage in extramarital affairs. These men are often chivalrous when it comes to their mistresses.

Many married men present themselves as nice guys that are unhappy in their marriage but are often unhappy within themselves. These men want women to be sympathetic to their needs. If you are dating a married man, he is more than likely dating more than just you. Most women that date married men rarely expect to marry these men. If you are dating a married man, be aware that you may one day want marriage. One should only do unto others what they want done unto them. The women that unknowingly date married men are often disappointed in the end. The wives are often used to their husbands' behavior. If she married him, she accepted him for who he is. A woman is typically able to identify if a man is married because he will rarely be available. These men rarely tell you where they live, or allow you to meet their family, or invite you out. If you are dating a guy like this, there is a possibility that he is married. There are married men that fall in love with other women and leave their wives for those women.

Men mainly leave their wife when their needs are not being met at home. Ladies, if you are married, and are meeting your man's needs, this does not apply to you. If you provide your man with what he needs, and he is being unfaithful, it is most likely a self-esteem issue. You know your husband and why he does what he does.

Some men use excuses for their behavior. He could believe the grass is greener on the other side. He may just need attention. The reasons men cheat are endless. Your man will be the only one to truly explain why infidelity was an option for him. Keep in mind that if you are dating a married man, he has a lack of respect for boundaries. His lack of respect for his wife shows his value of marriage. If he has a lack of respect for his union, it is also possible that he may have a lack of respect for you.

Regardless of the type of married man that you date, he is still a married man. Could you really be with him? You must be able to answer that. Your insight is important in your decision making. If you are not making good decisions for yourself, then what kind of decisions are you making? There have been many women scorned after dating married men and were confused on why. If a man shows you who he is, do not make excuses for his behavior. You must believe what is presented before you. When you make excuses, you are accepting his behavior.

You are offering him the green light to repeat the trend. You must do what you are comfortable with. What he does affects everyone around him. What you accept affects everyone around you. It is important to decipher what kind of energy you want in your life.

As a woman, you must identify where your accountability lies. If you are dating a married man, and you are in love with him, how does the story end? Well, the story can end many ways. If he leaves his wife, does the wife go peacefully? Every way will constitute some type of drama associated with it. Ultimately, the decision is yours. You will have to deal with whatever comes with your choices. Let us not forget that he may cheat on you too. Most women rarely realize that if the man leaves one woman for the next best thing, he will often leave that woman too. Many women dating married men love the ability to be able to send him home. Regardless of if this is true or not, his honor is his loyalty.

A man that is loyal will not stray when there is disruption in his relationship. An honorable married man will be definitive about his position to love his wife and work through any turmoil. An upstanding husband with integrity will respect the vows that he took. A man that is flighty is a man that is never satisfied. You can tell that he is not satisfied if he is cheating on his wife. Ladies, do yourself a favor and leave the married men to their wives. Allow them to deal with who they are committed to. There are enough single men to choose from, rather than wait for something that may never happen. You neither want the drama nor do you need the karma.

You may be dating a married man for many reasons but if you are in this situation, it may be best to choose you. He is already committed to someone else. If you are having a difficult time trying to leave, here are a few steps that may help. 1. Go a week without contact. This means that you need to block him from all devices and social media pages. 2. Do not answer blocked calls. 3. Stay busy often, which may include focusing on hobbies. 4. Do not check his social media pages, look at pictures, re-read text messages, listen to love songs, or reminisce about this man. 5. Self-reflect. This means that you need to spend time thinking about what you want for yourself. This includes what kind of man you want, how you want to be treated and what you truly deserve. 6. Keep up the good work. If you can go a week and your life feels fuller, and you are happier, then you are doing something right. Why not continue to do what makes you feel good? It is normal to miss someone that you were once with but it is important to let him go if he is not good for you. You can also use this process for men in other categories.

If you are in this situation and are capable to move on, then move on. Know your worth and know what you want. If you are involved with a married guy, it is probably not best to remain friends once the relationship is over. It is often best to severe ties because men love to keep communication lines open. It could be easy to revert to your previous behaviors and restart the cycle. A man will not be able to commit to you while betraying his union.

Do you want a man that is betraying his union or one that honors his commitment? You must decide. Anytime you have a situationship with an unavailable guy, you are subjecting yourself to sharing. If you share a man, you will probably always have to share him. Set a standard. If you are a married woman reading this chapter, and you feel like your husband is cheating, seek counseling, try to identify the problems and resolve them within your relationship. There is no perfect relationship in the world.

Relationships take dedication and work. You must decide if you want to remain in your marriage. Marriage is not as easy to separate yourself from as it is if you are a single woman. You may have children together. You may share businesses together. You must determine what is best for you and your family.

If you want your marriage to work, you must put effort. There is a possibility that you can reconcile. If you have tried to reconcile and he does not want to, you have a decision to make. You must determine if he wants what you want. His actions will show you if he wants to fight for his marriage. Create a list of your needs and wants in a man. Decide if you are willing to sacrifice a need for a want. The more time a woman spends away from her marriage, the clearer her vision will be. A woman that allows herself time and space will be able to process her feelings and her needs. Every relationship that you enter will provide you with a new experience and lesson. New experiences and lessons will teach you things that you will use throughout life.

Marriage is a sacred union that two people join. These individuals vow to protect and care for each other until the end of their lives. Some individuals are not as respectful of the union as they should be. More marriages are lasting longer than ever before, which constitutes hope for the culture. Marriages can last if unions are respected. If unions are disregarded, it could cause chaos, dysfunction and confusion. If you are not married, would you want another woman to disregard your marriage?

If more women respect the foundations of marriage, it will reduce the ability for married men to cheat. How can a man cheat if there is no one to cheat with? If you set high standards for yourself, men will not be able to disrespect you when they disrespect themselves. Some women have issues committing to men because of behaviors seen in marriages around them. The behavior that you see should not deter you from love and marriage. The behavior you witness is to teach you what not to do to ensure success in your marriage. Unfaithful men will always test their boundaries.

Every woman has a capacity of what she is willing to endure. A man that loves you will work hard to keep you. He will not have a wife, cheat on you or disrespect you. The man that chooses you will try to ensure that you are happy at all costs. You bring joy and happiness wherever you go. The man that is courting you is someone that you allowed in your life. The choices that you make for yourself should be with purpose and dignity. A man will always come along. The key is to only allow the right man in.

CHAPTER SIX

The Sugar Daddy

Most sugar daddies are marriage material. A sugar daddy seems to be the answer to all your prayers. Sugar daddies are often older men that prefer dating younger women. Many of these men are affluent. These men often shower you with gifts. Sugar daddies attempt to use their money and power to entice women. Many sugar daddies have self-esteem issues. These issues prevent them from maintaining healthy relationships with women. Sugar daddies often control women with monetary gifts. He will want marriage and family, but his woman may want something else. This may delay his marriage. His issue with commitment stems from personal issues within himself.

Early in the relationship, most Sugar daddies use chivalrous gestures to lure you in. Sugar daddies ultimately want love, but often have a difficult time expressing their feelings. Sugar Daddies need women to be dependent on them. Not all Sugar Daddies are older guys. Some Sugar Daddies are within your age range. Sugar Daddies are often men that use money to control those around them.

Your Sugar Daddy will give you just enough money for you to become accustomed to a certain lifestyle, but not enough to acquire the lifestyle without him. These men care for women financially, but many women are not satisfied with this lifestyle. The lifestyle often comes at a price. The price is often your self-dignity. Women have openly discussed the abuse experienced in relationships with men surrounding wealth and power. These men often want to select your friends and control your time. Does this sound familiar? Sugar Daddies are not the only men that try to control the woman that they are with. Sugar Daddies are more often the most difficult to deal with. Ladies, if you are in a relationship like this, it is important to understand and request what you need. If you absolutely love him, and he loves you, it should be simple. If a man loves you, he will show you by his actions.

You should receive thoughtful gifts in a relationship, but you should also receive respect. If he does not respect you, he does not value you. The promotion of therapy is necessary in any situation where there is some sort of discord. My suggestion is to attempt therapy to improve your relationship quality. If therapy does not improve your relationship, you have a decision to make.

If your relationship is volatile, and you are afraid to leave, contact your local domestic violence hotline for assistance. Every state has one. Some women are in dangerous relationships and are afraid to leave their man. If you are in a situation like this, reach out to a friend for support and seek help. You have a right to happiness and if your man is unwilling to try to make you happy, you must do what is best for you. Sugar Daddies can become overbearing since they are investing their money in their women. Many women may have resentments with their sugar daddies. Relationships with Sugar Daddies are often seen as propositional relationships. He is willing to provide something if she is willing to offer something. What does it value a woman to gain monetarily and to lose herself in the process?

How he treats you is how he regards you. How he makes you feel is how you perceive yourself. If you love him, attempt to identify the barriers that prevent your relationship from being as successful as possible. Sugar Daddies target younger women because older women have more experience with men. Older women have experienced marriage and have children. The men that want power over a woman will attempt to control their every move. Have you given up anything that you want to do? There is rarely any compromise with sugar daddies.

It is often their way or else. Why do younger women date older men? Is it for a sense of protection and security? Do you believe they are more mature than the men your age? Whatever the reason, men come with baggage. The older the man, the more baggage he will have. Be sure that you are prepared for it. Prior to a relationship with a sugar daddy, identify what he expects from you. Sugar daddies are aware that younger women come with less baggage than older women. Some younger women are reluctant to date men their age. Just remember that exposing yourself to an older man will make you mature faster than if you dated a man your age. If you are dating a sugar daddy and you are happy in your relationship, keep working towards your goal.

If you are unhappy with your sugar daddy, and he is too overbearing, have a discussion with him. A person can't understand what you need if you don't express it. Explain how his behavior makes you feel. Also, identify if he is willing to attend counseling. Men are initially reluctant to counseling but understand the benefits once they attend. Women are in relationships with sugar daddies for many reasons. One of the biggest reasons is for financial stability. Women often complain about men their age being unstable and immature. Many young women fall in love with older men. The relationship often ends in turmoil.

You will always endure some type of pain in a relationship. People sometimes hurt your feelings unintentionally. Men are strategic when they select a wife. Sugar daddies often marry women that they can control. If he can control you, he does not have to worry about you. Many men are insecure and need control to feel secure. If he is controlling but not overbearing, this could be something that you can address. Some women love having a protective man. Nobody is perfect. You must be imperfectly perfect for one another. Determine if his goals align with yours. If a man is dating you, it is because he feels that you complement him, but that should not be his only reason for dating you. He should be interested in your likes and dislikes.

Your aspirations and ambitions should be important to him. He should feel that you bring out the best in him, and vice versa. He should also support your dreams. If he does not support your dreams, then you must ask yourself what you are doing. If you are dating, make sure you are interested in getting to know the man to determine if there is a possibility for growth. If you are dating a sugar daddy and he embarrasses you in front of others, or does anything else demeaning, please think about your future.

Can you marry a man that is irrational? Women are living in unhealthy relationships where they are being emotionally and physically abused. These women rarely think about the long-term effects of abuse. If you are in an abusive relationship, and feel that you can't leave, please reach out to your local hotline for domestic violence. Some men suffer from childhood trauma and display it in adulthood. Therefore, women should get to know a man before entering a relationship with him or becoming intimate. It is easy to get into a relationship but difficult to let it go. She should never move in with a man, unless she wants to marry him.

Research has shown that cohabitation drastically reduces the chance of marriage. If you are with a sugar daddy and he loves you, inspires you, and does not try to control you, you have a great mate. If not, you must determine what is best for you. People have been known to remain in loveless marriages for their children to have two-parent family dynamics until their children were adults. You determine what you want for your life. Your life is for you to live. If you have children, you must consider them above all else. My impression of the philosopher was one of admirability. The courage to remain unhappy for the happiness of your children is extremely selfless.

Every relationship is not as fortunate when children are involved. Some parents must separate for the well-being of their children. Some people are selfish and rarely consider the children. A woman should always feel loved and supported in her relationship. A man constantly apologizing for his behavior but refusing to change is a man that is not ready for you. A woman lowering her standards and accepting anything less, increases a man's ability to increase his negative behavior. You should never feel afraid, unappreciated, or abused in your relationship, regardless of what he says you have done. Love yourself and set the expectation of how he should love you. If he is unable to love you the way you need to be loved, you have a decision to make.

The way that you love others also sets a standard for this man. You force him to notice how you love others and how you want your love reciprocated. What you want from a relationship is what you should receive. Relationships are about compromise. Relationships are not dictatorships that are solely controlled by one individual. That is not happiness.

Are you falling in love with the wrong men continuously and wondering why? You may be looking for love in all the wrong places and from all the wrong people. When you are single, some may associate being single with loneliness and failure. Being single is associated with strength and faith, not loneliness or failure. There has always been a negative connotation with being single. Being single and happy is always better than being miserable and in a relationship. Life is too short to be stressed or depressed. Some women allow society to dictate when a woman should wed or begin a family. It is important to wait until you are ready for love. Love is hard. Love is real. Love is not something for the immature.

When you rush into a relationship, you could be making a careless mistake. You must know what kind of man you want before you decide to enter a relationship. You should ask yourself what you are genuinely looking for in a man. The question is important because the answer is different for every woman. This book is here to assist you with the ability to differentiate between a meaningful relationship and a meaningless one.

We discuss ways to identify patterns in relationships. We focus on how self-empowerment, self-love, self-acceptance and self-growth are powerful tools for establishing your worth and how men can destroy them if you are not careful. Men rarely acknowledge how much power they have over their women. Women rarely understand how traumatized they are until a relationship is over. Some women transfer their post-traumatic stress into a new relationship, which causes major dilemmas in growth & development. You must learn to let go and grow. You may need therapy to recover. Whatever assistance you need, ask for it. The people around you are your support system. Those people love you. Ask for what you want from your man. If he is willing to provide what you need, then he is the man for you. If not, then he isn't. Life is simple. We make it complicated.

CHAPTER SEVEN

The Ex

There is no woman in the world that does not have an ex. An ex or ex-boyfriend is a guy that you have dated or were in a relationship with, and the relationship ended for one reason or another. There is often a connection between the two that interferes with the woman's ability to move on. She knows who her ex is. He may have hurt her in the past, but she knows what to expect from him. A woman usually dates her ex-boyfriend when she is in between relationships. Some women date an ex-boyfriend while dating a new boyfriend. Ex-boyfriends never want to let you go, so they rarely mind competition. Your ex often treats you as if you are the number one woman in his life, which may be the furthest thing from the truth.

Your ex may treat you better than your current man. He is attentive to your needs. He focuses on your words and tells you what you want to hear. Ex-boyfriends seem to get everything right, but women often know it is an illusion. Ex-boyfriends attempt to sabotage any relationship that you attempt to develop with someone new. Your ex-boyfriend will more often play the role of a best friend.

He will want all the benefits of the relationship without the title. Single women are comfortable with their exes. You may contact him or a regular basis. You may tell him everything. Your ex-boyfriend will want to cater to your needs to reduce your need for your new boyfriend. Women associate comfort with intimacy and are rarely intimate with individuals they are not comfortable with. Women continue to crave intimacy while single. Ex-boyfriends will take advantage of that if you allow them to. Your ex is your ex for a reason. Unless you are attempting to rekindle your romance, what is your purpose of going backwards? If he could not love you when he was with you, how much power should he have over your future?

A man will not want you but will not want another man to have you. Does that mean he is ready to love you properly? You can determine if he has changed by his actions. Some men people pretend to change, but just learn to mask their behavior. Ultimately, you decide if you want to give your ex a second chance. My perception is that if you give him an opportunity to show you that he has changed, his actions should reflect intent, not apologies. Many women have taken exes back and noticed that the behavior they left for had magnified.

Be knowledgeable about what you want for yourself will imperatively shape your relational paradigm. What you are taught about love only shows half the portrait. The beauty of the photo rarely reflects the dedication that was required to make the masterpiece. Every woman wants marriage, but is every woman willing to put in the work? Every man wants a companion but are they all willing to do what it takes to acquire the companionship that they genuinely want? Some individuals settle for those that love them. If one settles in their relational paradigm, the other individual may suffer because the person you are with may want to be with someone else.

A woman that has ended a relationship with an ex, has decided to move on. If she continues reliving the past, she must identify the reasons why. Some women are afraid of starting over. Some women are afraid of being hurt again. Many women keep an ex around for convenience. When a woman is dating an ex, she will most often continue to see him until her new man ends the relationship. Your ex-boyfriend is often aware if you still harbor feelings for him. He may use that to his advantage. Be leery of what you are returning to your ex for. Your ex-boyfriend is happy with you being in limbo. If you are in limbo with him, you will not be able to focus on re-branding yourself.

Your ex-boyfriend will not be pursuing you like he did when he met you. You will often only see him when he is available. Your ex-boyfriend will be in a new relationship while you are holding onto him. If you are dating your ex-boyfriend, you must ask yourself what you are you trying to gain. Why did you end the relationship? If the answer to the question has anything to do with his lack of effort, then why have you revisited the relationship? Some individuals may never be able to provide you with what you need, so when do you stop giving them that option?

Regardless of if you are willing to provide a man multiple chances to show you that he is ready for commitment, when does it end? Ex-boyfriends rarely commit to their ex-girlfriends. They often portray themselves as friends but are primarily focused on benefits. This even applies when children are involved. Many exes enjoy their space and are not looking for commitment.

Your ex made excuses and that is often why you left. He was unable to commit to you. He often blamed you for the relationship failing. If you are dating your ex, you should have minimal expectations of him. If you keep your expectations to a minimum, it will be more difficult for him to disappoint you. You must determine if his behavior has changed or if he is the same man you left.

If you are trying to transform him, you will learn quickly that a man will only change when he is ready. Women maintain relationships with their exes for many reasons. Identify what your reasons are and determine if he is worth it. You could end up being resentful when you could have ended things amicably and kept a friend. To discover what you want in a man may not be an easy plight. You will realize that finding yourself is more important. When one relationship ends, you need time and space to rejuvenate your energy. When you let go of what was, you can begin to focus on what can be. You will learn that being single is the key to growth. You will realize that love starts from within and while in a relationship, you rarely focused on yourself.

When you are in a relationship, you are focused on the relationship. When you are single, you can spend time identifying what you want in a man. You can also identify common errors that you made. Self-love is imperative to a healthy mental state. A man can make a woman feel unwanted and unloved, which may affect her self-esteem. Women rarely share these feelings with anyone. They tend to be embarrassed and associate a failed relationship with failure. Just because the relationship failed does not make you a failure.

One must fail at one relationship to recognize the right one. When a relationship ends, it is best if a woman remains single for at least six months. Some women may feel that waiting six months is extreme. Let us break down the six-month transition period. For the first month, you should occupy your time with things you enjoy doing. For the second month, you should occupy your time doing things that will further your career. For the third month, you should start going to the gym, begin eating healthier and identify why your relationship ended. For the fourth month, you should purchase a few new outfits, plan a vacation with your friends and decide what you learned from the break-up. For the fifth month, continue to exercise, purchase a few self-help books, read the self-help books and begin practicing things you learned. For the sixth month, re-read the self-help books and travel with your friends.

By the time you complete your six-month transition period, you will be ready to move on emotionally from your ex. You will realize during the six months apart from your ex that you have acquired some of their personality traits. You need time to release him from your system. The time that you take for yourself is necessary to focus on your needs. If you are not where you need to be, how can you be good to anyone around you?

Once you have given yourself an appropriate amount of time to heal, you will have a new mindset and be ready for love. Reflection time is necessary. Be patient with yourself or you will make mistakes. Exes are exes for a reason. Whether you were incompatible or timing interfered, you are not with him. You are not with him because you are not supposed to be with him. What is meant to be will be. When a woman can identify why she dated her ex, she will be able to understand why she no longer wants to. Once you re-evaluate your relationship, you can then decide if you really want it back. Reaching out to an ex often goes nowhere fast and how does it affect your current relationship? Your ex may reach out to you to rekindle the flame, reminisce on the past, or to stroke his ego. Either way, this distraction could cloud your judgement or affect your new relationship, which is why it is important to be ready to move on.

A new man will not take you seriously if you are still involved with your ex. Why create problems for yourself when you had rid yourself of your ex? Women love the superficial attention that exes provide. If his attention is superficial, why would you want it? For you to give the best possible version of yourself, you must spend time by yourself.

Why allow someone to prevent you from moving on when they have no interest in a future with you? Being able to identify when an individual is being self-serving will show you their purpose. Identify if you are dating an ex for a self-fulfilling purpose. Being accountable is being aware of one's own actions and the consequences. Make decisions that will provide the best outcomes for your life.

CHAPTER EIGHT

Mr. Co-Dependent

Women love Co-Dependent men. Mr. Co-Dependent is the guy that loves to be in relationships. Mr. Co-Dependent loves love. Mr. Co-Dependent is the man that you parade around your friends. Women marry co-dependent men. Co-dependent men are often men with Type B personalities. These men are often nonchalant but confident. Mr. Co-Dependent despises dysfunction and needs order. Mr. Co-Dependent wants to be adored. Many co-dependent men get married multiple times throughout their lifetime. A co-dependent guy often jumps in and out of relationships because hates being alone. Women that are in positions of power love co-dependent men. Co-dependent men are often submissive by nature. Men associate submissiveness with femininity, but women associate it with humility.

Men that are submissive, tend to cater to their women's needs. Gender roles indicate that males and females have different roles. Men that apply gender roles in their relationship are often considered to be traditional and old-fashioned in accordance with responsibilities. These men are often domineering in their relationships. Dominant traditional men are often poised and perfectionist.

Many women struggle in relationships with these men. Perfect is often never perfect enough. Submissive men compliment your outfit while dominant men often ask you to change. In graduate school, my professor asked if my class thought that opposites attract. Our class had different opinions, but many indicated that opposites do attract. My professor indicated that people that are similar are more compatible than those that are opposite. Use these tips to assess if your man is your opposite: Identify 1. Priorities 2. Personality

Co-dependent men are different from men in the other categories because they are sensitive to their woman. The only way that a relationship could go wrong with a co-dependent man is if a woman wants an independent man. Women that love co-dependent men feel empowered by them. To feel empowered is to feel liberated. Some co-dependent men are often sensitive men. Co-dependent men are sometimes indecisive and need assistance with decisions. Some co-dependent men in relationships with independent women can feel emasculated.

Since these men are more in tune with their feminine side, some women misconstrue their kindness for weakness. Co-dependent men are strong and confident but yearn for a woman's reassurance.

Some women love men like this while other women reject men like this. If you are with Mr. Co-Dependent, how are you being treated? Are you happy? Throughout this book, we have discussed how men treat women in relationships. The chapter on Mr. Co-dependent focuses more on women's behaviors and actions as opposed to men. If a woman dates a co-dependent man and she wants a man that is more independent, she may end up frustrated with her man. Women often want men that are confident, so it can be overwhelming if you are with a man that needs constant reassurance. Another woman may feel as though she has attained the total package. The difference between the two women is what kind of woman they are.

Do you need to be in control in your relationship? If you need control, you and your co-dependent man could be a perfect match. If you need a man, to make the decisions in the relationship, a co-dependent man would not be your most compatible match. It takes great patience to be with a co-dependent man. Ladies that are in relationships with co-dependent men are often happy women. Some women believe that these men are weak, but these men are indeed strong. Any man that asks his woman what she needs to be happy, and strives to attain it, is a man that is willing to go to great lengths for his woman.

Do you want a man that is serious about you or one that plays games? If he is a bit too clingy, you can set some boundaries to teach him that you can love each other while enjoying space. Co-dependent men cater more to your needs than the men in the other categories. He caters to his woman, because he yearns for her adoration and understands that listening to her is the key to his happiness. Men in some of the other categories we discussed have different views on the value of women in their life. Co-dependent men are often more monogamous than men in the other categories. Co-dependent men put their women on a pedestal. These men are often extremely dependent and will want to spend all their available free time with you. Co-dependent men rarely want you to spend time with anyone other than them.

Many women love co-dependent men but often want to change things about them. The issue with trying to change a man is that you cannot. You are not in a relationship to try to change anyone. Your attempt to change him will heighten his need for freedom. You are in a relationship for companionship. The only person that you have power over is yourself. The only person that you can change is yourself. You must love him for who he is or let him go.

You can want your man to compromise for you, but he should never have to compromise himself. If you are unhappy in your relationship, it is best to re-evaluate your decision to be in the relationship. There is someone for everybody. You would never want anyone to require you to change to be with them. If his co-dependency is suffocating you, discuss it in a way that doesn't insult him. Tell him that you need personal time to tend to your self-care needs. He should be able to understand that. If he has an issue with giving you space, you must do what is best for you. A co-dependent man is willing to do what it takes to make you happy but attempting to change his personality will ignite major resistance.

Remember these two rules when dating co-dependent men 1. Never attempt to emasculate him. He will resent you 2. Remain honest about your feelings. Mr. Co-dependent will always respect the truth over a lie. If you believe you met your soulmate, try giving the relationship your all. This means you should love him wholeheartedly. If your man treats you like a queen, supports you, is dependable and shows you adoration, he is the man you should marry. The value of marriage has diminished over the years. Marriages end when people fail to honor their vows of commitment to their spouse. Not everyone is ready for marriage at the same time.

If you disregard your union or someone else's, do you think yours will be respected? Lead by example. Perfect yourself until the right man comes along. Mr. Co-dependent should not be treated like any other man that is single. Mr. Co-dependent is husband material so be honest with him. Women fall in love with co-dependent men because their love inspires and supports all their aspirations. It would be difficult to not fall in love with Mr. Co-dependent. Mr. Co-dependent is a great provider. His focus is for you to shine. This man will provide you a companionship that you never felt before.

You will understand why it failed with everyone else. Some women tend to find interest in men that show minimal interest in them. Why? The individual giving you what you need is the man that loves you. Any man can give you what you want but if you are also able to attain what you need for growth, this man is worth serious consideration.

Love is a feeling that can change in an instant but if two people are able to grow together, their love could last a lifetime. Relationships fail due to deception, infidelity and mostly financial issues.

Love for some is conditional. When you meet an individual, it is imperative to pace yourself during the courtship process. A relationship should only transpire when you are truly ready to commit. Your mindset of readiness to commit will be established based upon your timeline. You should not feel pressure to commit. You should not pressure anyone to commit to you. It is important to be able to identify what you want from your man and what you want out of a relationship before commitment. Two people must be able to compromise for their relationship to work, and that takes time to learn.

It takes more than six months to learn your partner. It is important to take things slow with a man. If you move too fast, you will miss the chance to get to know him. You may be intimate before you have realized that he is self-centered and ungrateful. Everyone has a different personality when you meet them that changes during the relationship. Is the man that you are dating going to be your husband? You could ask yourself; does he want children? How does he treat his mother? Is he thoughtful? To answer the questions, you must learn about your man. While you are getting to know your man, you are also trying to identify if this is someone that you could share your life with. Every woman has different needs from her man.

You also want to identify if you have similar wants in life. Ladies, we tend to talk more than we listen, but the key to learning is listening. Key 3: You perfect yourself, until the right man comes along. Pay attention to his actions. His actions will show you how he feels about you. It is not important to discuss your exes and what went wrong in your previous relationships. Keep your history in the past because if you fail to do so, it may be used against you later. You are dating to enjoy his company. Since people rarely show you who they are when you start dating, you should take your time getting to know him to ensure he is the guy for you.

CHAPTER NINE

Your Dream Guy

Your Dream Guy is the man from your dreams. He will love you beyond limits and have every quality that you want in a man. This guy will be your protector, confidant, best friend and soul partner. He will be everything that has been absent in your life. You will not have to force a relationship with your dream guy. He will exceed every expectation that you have set for any man. This man will not be like any other man that you have dated. You will be able to be yourself with this man. He will uplift you, empower you, educate you, and most of all, love you. He will not change once you fall in love. You will not have to compromise yourself or your dignity to be with this man. He will show you that he is serious about you by the way he takes interest in every aspect of your life. He will want you to meet his family.

Your dream guy will discuss a future with you and incorporate you into his life. His vision will encompass yours so intensely, that you will know you have found true love.

If your man does not meet the above, he is not your dream guy. Your dream guy will be like you. He will want what you want from life. He will be the ying to your yang. You will be able separate this man from any other man because this relationship will be easy. This relationship will flourish. He will give you space and not consume all your time. He will understand that you have other responsibilities and obligations, and never make you feel guilty for spending time away from home. The butterflies will not fade after a year of dating. The butterflies increase with the time that you share with him. This man will not attempt to change you. You will not attempt to change this man. This man will bring out the best in you. He will be able to admit that he is wrong. He will always be honest with you. This man will not be perfect, but you will love his imperfections. This man is often unattainable for many.

If a woman is not prepared to accept love, she may miss her dream guy. You must be ready for your dream man to allow him in. Many women are afraid of being vulnerable when they meet their dream man and lose him because of it. If you are between relationships, or hurt from a previous relationship, it could interfere with your opportunity to accept your dream guy. For you to experience true love, you must let your guard down.

Not every man that you meet will be the right man for you. You decide if this man is worthy of your time. Relationships end if they are not strong enough to withstand the test of time. Women are sometimes resentful if their relationships fail. If one resents a relationship, those feelings can hinder progress and growth. Does this apply to you? It is important to be open to growth to reduce the risk of engaging in re-occurring behaviors. Some women experience re-occurring issues with different men and question why it continuously occurs. Some women prosecute their new men for other men's behavior, hence the importance of dealing with any unresolved issues from a previous relationship before moving on.

Many women begin dating immediately after a relationship ends to occupy their time. It is important to understand that you are not ready to date and should remain single before you miss out on something spectacular while wallowing over something useless. Women are the strongest creatures on earth. Women carry many titles and are often held responsible for the success of their relationship. Being responsible for the success of a relationship puts a lot of pressure on women. If you are not with your dream man; is your relationship tumultuous? Are you in a loving relationship? Does you beau meet the criteria you want in a man?

Do you hold your man accountable for his actions? Do you hold yourself accountable for your actions? Some women have a difficult time addressing accountability. In relationships, people often want to blame the other individual for the relationship failing. If you blame your partner, what are you learning? Your partner will learn from his mistakes and you will learn from yours. Some women encountered parental discord during childhood. How do you think your childhood influences how you interact with your partner? Take a moment to think about this. What experiences from your childhood have shaped your ideas of love? Many experiences that you have witnessed and endured have contributed to your choices in men and with men.

Therefore, it is important to understand why you choose who you choose. It is not important to just understand your family love dynamic, it is also important to understand your mates. Discuss your man's upbringing with him in depth, before marriage & family. If you rush into a relationship for companionship, you may find yourself miserable in it. If you are dating a man and you must excuse behaviors for him, he is not your dream guy. While you are single, you should be preparing for your dream guy.

The only way to prepare for your dream guy is by perfecting yourself. You need to be in a space where your past burdens have been released before you can accept your dream guy. The way to become the best version of yourself is by investing time in yourself. As women, you carry so many responsibilities that you often neglect yourself. You can begin creating a better version of yourself by selecting better eating habits and implementing a daily workout in your routine. Pamper yourself with massages and hair and nail appointments. Travel the world with your friends. Try things that you have always wanted to do, like acting, or singing. When you are self-reflecting, you will notice that you are extremely busy and rarely feel lonely.

Patience and selectiveness are a priority when choosing the right partner. Be patient. The right man will come along. You just need to pay attention. Enjoy yourself. When you step out of your front door, understand that dozens of men will be interested in you. Do you choose them all? If you start a relationship with the first guy you meet, you may be disappointed when it is over. If you have read through this book, you will have realized that if you continuously apply the same rules, you will continue to see the same results. Therefore, it is important to find yourself while you are single.

Remember, you are single for a reason. Follow these two rules faithfully while single: 1. While you are single, spend some spare time identifying what went wrong in your last relationship. 2. Identify what you need from a relationship. When a woman identifies her own flaws, she can begin addressing them. What went wrong in your previous relationship was not only your ex's fault. You were not perfect either. Once you have conquered your flaws, you will be prepared to move on. You can casually date until you find someone that truly meets your expectations. When you met a man that interests you, you need to provide him with a clean slate. You should never bring your old insecurities and baggage to this new friendship/relationship. You should never mistreat him because you are not ready for a relationship. This can be extremely difficult for some.

You must be open to love when you meet this man. Some women are afraid to love because of past experiences. Vulnerability is the only way to be able to love unconditionally. Most women are aware that if you are vulnerable, your man can hurt you. One should be selective on who they choose to love. Your dream man would never hurt you. When people have been hurt, it is often difficult to trust again. You will only cheat yourself if you fear love.

If you are struggling with any of the areas above, therapy may be something to explore. Some relationships cause post-traumatic stress for women and men. If you are in a relationship that is valuable and therapy appears appealing, bring your partner with you. There are therapists that provide an array of services to couples that support their relationship to assist around trust issues, commitment & love. One of the biggest secrets to making a relationship flourish is to put everything into it. If you are mistreating someone, or someone is mistreating you, is that your best effort? If you are unable to love because you are in pain, stop trying to. You will hurt yourself in the process of searching for love in all the wrong places.

Throughout the book, we focused on men. We rarely focused on behaviors women exhibit. A woman must put forth the same effort that she requires from her man. If you want a man to take you seriously, you must show him that you are serious. This can be difficult for women that have unresolved pain. That is why therapy is important for some to move forward.

One must allow themselves the ability to have blind faith to ensure nothing can stand in the way of love. When two people give their all to each other, they are unstoppable together.

If you are single, and are truly ready for commitment, you are ready for your dream guy. Your dream guy will be considerate, able to communicate, ready for commitment and will treat you like you've never been treated before. When you meet your dream man, do not fail to cease the opportunity because you are not ready for love. Be ready, willing and able for what you deserve.

CHAPTER TEN

You

Identifying who you are is the most important aspect of your relationship with anyone. If you are indecisive about your wants, then other people will have the ability to influence your thoughts. You determine what you want in your life emotionally, physically and spiritually. The man that you choose to be in a relationship with speaks volumes about who you are and what you genuinely want. Women will say they want one thing but need something else. The man that you choose to share your time with is important. This man could potentially be your husband. The man that you choose also portrays your direction in life. If you have children, is your man the best example for your children? Regardless of if your man is the father of your children or not, he should set a good example for them.

Your perception of a relationship in adulthood is influenced by your experiences throughout life. Therefore, it is imperative to identify any issues that you have experienced in childhood and discover how it relates to your actions in your relationships as an adult.

For example, as a youth, a woman grew up neglected by her parents, and as an adult, she yearns for adoration. The type of adoration that she is yearning for will never be fulfilled by a man, hence the reoccurring issues with the men she dates. Use the exercise below to determine your reflective patterns with men. The reflection pattern exercise will show you how to identify your repetitive patterns in relationships.

Reflection Pattern Exercise

Write down the names of every man that you ever thought you loved. Once you have written the names down, next to each name, list the reason(s) your relationship ended. Identify if there is a pattern and write it down? Do you notice any patterns that need to be broken? Do you ever recall dating a man and realizing early on that he was not the man for you, but you continued to see him anyway? Many women think they can change their man. A woman must understand that it is not her responsibility to change her man. It is up to him to want change. Nobody can make a better choice for you, than yourself. You alone are in control of changing yourself. If the man that you are with is not the man for you, he will not change, because that it what you are requesting. He is going to be the man that he wants to be.

If he is interested in changing, it will be when he is ready to change. You must make the best choices for your life when choosing your partner. Your happiness is at stake. You should not play games with your life. If you want to play, understand that you may not win in the end. Games often end with a sore loser. You must be unwavering and definitive about what you want in your life. Women rarely need confirmation, just conviction. He is either the right or the wrong man for you, but only you will truly know.

Since your experiences shape your behavior, how many of those behaviors have you exhibited in your relationships? We all develop a sense of who we are from our parents. We also develop our differences from our parents. When we become adults, we rarely think about how our experiences impact our relationships. We all derive from various family dynamics that influence our upbringing. How was the relationship quality between your parents? How is the quality of your relationship with your man? How many of your childhood experiences can you attribute your relationship quality as an adult to?

History develops us, and our experiences influence our decisions. In some relationships, women often focus more on their partners than themselves.

The responsibility of being the glue in a family can be overwhelming at times. If you need an outlet, many jobs offer an employment assistance programs which provide free counseling sessions to employees. Some women may believe that counseling is unnecessary, but many find it beneficial. If you feel that you have compartmentalized your emotions subconsciously, therapy will assist you with destroying those barricades that prevent true happiness. Support is often necessary in the process of growth. Utilize this exercise to determine your latent love pattern. The latent love pattern will show you how to identify patterns in your behavior.

Identifying your latent love pattern:

Write down five lessons that you learnt from your parent's relationship quality. Ex: My mother was extremely supportive to my father. My father was very thoughtful when it came to my mother. Do not write down what your parents told you. Write down what you observed. Once you complete that, write down how many of those things you have done in your relationship as an adult. Do you exhibit any of your parents' patterns in your own relationship? Are the behaviors that you exhibit from your parents often negative or positive? If you have any negative behaviors that you acquired from your parents, write them down.

Also write down every positive experience. Once you have written them down, you can discover how often you have previously displayed those characteristics in a relationship. Any negative behavior that you learnt can be unlearned. One must understand that a behavior exists before it can be changed. We rarely recognize the behaviors that we exhibit until others identify them. Once identified, defense mechanisms make some people deny the behavior without reflecting.

Those individuals are not ready for change. You can utilize the latent love pattern to identify behaviors that you are displaying and interested in changing. Manifest what you want in your life and it will appear. If you think negatively, negative things will happen. If you think positively, positive things will happen. We decide what holds value in our lives and hearts. If you are happy and in a good space, whether single or in a relationship, you will attract greatness. It will be easy to reject anything less than your worth. Love starts from within. You must first love yourself before those around you will love you and treat you accordingly. Your inward issues reflect outwardly, so it is helpful to identify them, learn, and grow from them. Many women begin a relationship when they are not ready. Make sure you are prepared to enter a relationship before committing.

If you are in a rush to start a family, discuss your options with your medical provider to be aligned with your biological clock. It is more important to be selective in choosing your husband. Choosing your life partner is not supposed to be a race. Marriage is something that should be weighed heavily. The individual that you decide to share your life with is the individual that you trust with your life. You must be certain the individual that you choose is honorable, has integrity and a great moral compass. If your consideration of marriage is as a result of words of affirmation or acts of service, ensure you are content with just that. Know of the personality of the individual that you are choosing to spend your life with. A man's personality is incredibly important when determining if he is marriage material.

Marriage is a full-time responsibility that one must be prepared for. It is your responsibility to determine what you are ready for. Being able to develop a balance for home and work can be overwhelming, and it can be a lot of pressure to ensure other responsibilities are not being neglected. If you choose family while developing yourself, it is important to make time for yourself. Many women in relationships lose themselves and feel cheated if the relationship ends.

You never want to have a battle between what you love and who you love. You want to make the best choices for yourself. Before you accept love, you must be ready for it. Your career will require a lot of your attention, but your man will require much more. You must have the ability to provide an equal amount of time to both. Before you start your family, you should have the time to focus on them. Women often feel guilty for spending hours away from home. Men can get restless in relationships where their women are focused on everything else except him.

Some women may feel that their man is too clingy or insecure. Other women may have difficulties striking a balance. A man can be supportive of your dreams but also feel neglected if he is not being included in them. If you can incorporate him in your other responsibilities, it may bring you closer together. If you are unable to incorporate him, your career and marriage could be in jeopardy. Some couples can engage in business and pleasure, but you should ensure your relationship can handle both. Some men despise when their women are unable to tend to their needs. If you are managing both roles, you must organize your time. It is all about what you can deal with.

If you are not providing your man with the appropriate amount of attention, he could potentially stray. This is not to scare you, because if a man genuinely wants you, you will never have to worry about another woman. If a man is for you, he will be all about you. You will date a few men before you find your husband. If you use the tools in this book, it will be easier for you to identify the right man for you. You will know when you meet this man because everything about the relationship will be organic. He will give you everything you need. He will be able to get along with your friends and your family. You will get along well with his family and his friends. You may not like all the same things, but compromising will not be difficult. He will enjoy doing what you like because he wants to make you happy.

You will also do what he likes to make him happy. You will treat him good because he treats you good. Being with him will not feel like an obligation or a bad decision. You will want to do any and everything to make this man happy. You will not feel like your love goes unnoticed. This relationship will be meaningful. This bond will be durable and long lasting. This man will not try to change you. This man will not try to use or abuse you. This man will only want to make you happy, encourage and provide for you.

You will notice that you are finally able to be yourself in a relationship. Many men introduce themselves as one man but are often truly someone else. You must determine if he is Mr. Right or Mr. Right now. You should be able to be your best self with this man. Lesson 4: If you are not enough, neither are they. If they are not enough, neither are you.

You should never have to change yourself or indicate that your partner needs to make changes for a relationship to prosper. You should only have to compromise choices not personalities. Let us explore the differences between compromise and change. A compromise is going to a restaurant that you may not like to appease your partner. When your partner tries to change you, he could ask you to be less sensitive.

You can compromise anything but yourself, just ensure that he is compromising as well. Let us look at this example: If you are sensitive, you have a right to be who you are. Why does your man want to change who you are? There are plenty sensitive men that love sensitive women. If you are being asked to compromise your dignity and personality, you will most likely suffer because you can't be yourself. An individual can change but it must be self-warranted. If you use manipulative tactics to incite change, your plan may backfire. Stand firm in your expectations. Love grows over time and is understanding.

Love is not perfect but will be the perfect love for you. Key 4: A man that offers true love, will not starve you of yourself. When you are ready for the man of your dream, avoid playing games with this man. Be honest, set the standard, and if he is worthy, risk it all.

CHAPTER ELEVEN

The Game

The main objective of the game is to play to win. The game is not for the timid. This chapter is for the women that want to learn or understand the game. The game is different for different people, but at some point, everyone will play. You may win or you may lose. Most people play the game in early adulthood. The game is often revealed through nature. You observe the game on television, in music, from family, and/or peers. People often play the game for many reasons. The rule of the game is to play before you get played. Some individuals play the game because they would rather hurt you than be hurt.

Your primary focus in the game is whatever objective you have for the man you are playing with. When playing the game, you date multiple people. There has been criticism associated with women playing the dating game. Men often refer to women that date multiple men with negative connotations. For a woman to decide if her boo is the right man, she must have something to compare him to. If a woman dates one man at a time, she limits herself to an experience that will assist her with the elimination process.

Men date more than one woman at a time before finding their wives. Women are available to do the same. If you make yourself readily available for the first man that shows you attention, then he chose you. Whether or not he chose you identifies your man's wants versus your own. If you chose him, you have decided that he has met all your standards as the perfect man for you. If you did not choose him, and he chose you, you will be trying to determine who you are dating your entire relationship. The game is not about dating multiple people. The game is not about playing with anyone's feelings. The game is about finding your perfect match. The game can be ruthless. Many individuals feel it is not important to be transparent if you are dating multiple people. My thoughts are honesty is the best policy. If you provide a choice to your partner, it allows them the ability to decide if they want to participate.

Women/Men tend to hide other friendships because they are afraid that it will limit their possibilities with the other individual. There is such a thing as too much too soon. It is also important to let an individual know what they are utterly agreeing to. Respect, Communication & Trust are three imperative factors for a relationship to prosper into marriage. If you begin a relationship with dishonesty, your relationship will be built on a lie.

If you are apprehensive about being honest, just try it. Honesty truly goes a long way. The option that you provide your partner is your agreement to the terms of your relationship. Some people take risks and are dishonest with their mates. If you play the game and utilize trickery to attain what you want, it could end in disaster. Being dishonest is never the appropriate way to get what you want. You can play the game while being truthful. If you manipulate people into falling in love, and you are not in love, you are playing unfairly. Fairness is the key to winning the right way. If you are not fair, the people around you will not be fair either. If you no longer want to play the game, it will be easier to stop if you were always honest. The game is the steppingstone to a relationship.

One of the individuals that you were playing with will become your partner. You want your partner to take you seriously. You want him to respect you, and for him to do that, you must respect yourself. The game is not something that you want in your relationship. The game is something you want to end before commitment. The game can hinder anything prosperous. The game interferes with trust and commitment. You must have trust for a relationship to flourish. An individual that you are unable to trust is not someone that you can give your all to. If the person you choose is unable to give his all to you, you lose.

If you begin with games, you will most often end with games. It is truly best not to play games at all. Games lead to destruction in relationships. You may be ready to stop playing but the man that you have been playing with is not. Where will that leave you? We model the behavior that we want exhibited. Let us take a moment to reflect. How many times have you met a man and he asked if you were single, you said no, and that man considered your relationship? You are probably unable to count the number of times that this has happened to you. Most men like competition. They are competitive by nature. Most men love the fact that other men want you. If you choose to play the game to find your soulmate, be honest with your prospective love candidate. You will notice that you may have some fun making your love interest a bit jealous when you are truthful. Just ensure that you are playing the game for love. If you are in the game for anything else, you may end up losing.

For women that hide the fact that they date multiple men, you should ask yourself why? If you are honest with him, he will be honest with you. You want your relationship to be built on honesty, even if it ends in friendship. It is better for a relationship to end amicably. If you notice that your love interest is showing a bit more attention, it is important to attribute some of his efforts to the other man.

When you choose your man, ensure that you choose based on his intentional actions to meet your needs. Your decision to date until you meet the right man is your choice. Once you determine if he is your soulmate, you can have a conversation about exclusivity.

It is important to be able to identify what you really want from a man before you delude him or he deludes you. The man of your dreams can be right in front of you but if you are playing the game, you may miss him.

Women spend too much time in unhappy/unhealthy relationships when they can create their own destiny. Since you create your own destiny, you decide who is worth your time and energy. You never have to be unhappy unless you want to. If you are yearning for companionship, ensure you remain selective.

You can date without having a toxic relationship. Relationships become toxic when individuals fail to respect boundaries. Playing the game, creates a tumultuous relationship. The games people play always have a consequence. When women meet men, they rarely reveal who they really are and vice versa. If you reveal your truest self to him, he will also reveal himself. As an example, follows. Men love to eat and a woman that hates cooking may pretend she loves to cook. When you pretend to be someone you are not, you will have to maintain that image.

Most individuals are unable to maintain a false image of themselves for long. Some individuals feel that if the relationship fails, it was a waste of time. Every lesson that you learn could never be a waste of time. You gain knowledge from every relationship. You determine if what you retained is useful. If you are in a relationship, it will continuously be tested, whether you are exclusive or in a situationship. If you have an open dialogue, you will be at an advantage to obtain information that you would not normally receive. The foundation that you build your relationship on will determine if it will be able to weather any storm.

The man that you choose should be a positive influence in your life. He should bring out things in you that you never thought you could achieve. He should make you laugh uncontrollably. You will know that he is the one because you want to spend every minute with this man. If you do not feel this way, there is no need to commit. If you want to build this, and your man is unwilling, you are wasting your time. Life is short to waste time. It is more important for you to enjoy your life, than to wait for someone to choose you.

Intimacy can incorporate drama in your relationship. Once a woman becomes intimate with a man, she often gains an emotional connection with him. Women are often only intimate with one man at a time.

When you decide that you want to take the relationship to the next level and become intimate, it is important to ask yourself if this man can be your husband. Being intimate often confuses things for women. Therefore, intimacy should only be had when you are ready. This is probably why our parents teach us to wait until marriage before intimacy. Ensure that the choices you make for your body are indeed for you. Most men encounter women and persuade them into intimacy. It is important for you to decide when you are ready for intimacy. When women become intimate too quickly, some regret it. Take your time to get to know your man before intimacy. Save yourself, until you truly know that he is the one. You want to know if your man is high on integrity and your morals align. You want to meet his family and friends to assess his relationships with others. You want to look at how he treats you.

Tell him who you are and what you want. If this guy wants something real with you, he will do things to show you that he wants you in his life. If you play the game, you will not be giving yourself a real chance at love. If you are honest and give him a fair chance at your heart, a relationship will progress. Many women sabotage new relationships because they have not unresolved issues from their past.

Some women rather play the game and appear happy than truly being happy. You never have to pretend to have love if you truly have it.

Real love does not have to be displayed to others for it to be true. The tarnished perceptions of publicized love often end in divorce. When you confirm happiness to others, people often attempt to test it. Perception is everything for some and nothing for others. Things that always appear appealing may not be the best thing for you. Would you rather have someone that appears to be good to you or someone that is genuinely good for you? Something that feels good will take time and effort but is often easy. Something that looks good, will always be abstract & complex and difficult to attain.

Why have something superficial when you can have something real? For you to have something real that will withstand the test of time, you must dedicate 100% of yourself into it. Are you giving your man 100%? Is he giving you 100%? There are theories that indicate relationships should be measured on a percentage scale, which explore who does the most for the other in the relationship. You determine the effort that you are willing to accept/and or give. Some indicate relationships should be 50/50. My opinion is that individuals must put in 100/100 to build an indestructible bond.

If you have identified what you want in a man, and you are ready to receive love, then opinions from others will not matter. Your man may not be a professional athlete, or social media personality. He may not be on the fifteen most handsome men in the United States list, but he is yours.

The man you choose reflects who you are, so choose wisely. Who you choose ends and begins with you.